Time and M

Catherine Twomey Fosnot

New Perspectives on Learning, LLC
1194 Ocean Avenue
New London, CT 06320

ISBN-13: 978-1-7335321-2-9

Table of Contents

Unit Overview

This unit is designed to be used after a prior grade one unit *The Timekeepers.* If that unit was not used prior and your students do not have a well-developed sense of the measurement of time regarding hours and half hours, you can combine the two units into one and use them together to make a 10 day unit. *The Timekeepers* was designed to develop an understanding of the need for standard units and an external timekeeping device to compare durations. Seconds and minutes were introduced with simple timers to allow students to experience short durations, and then hours were introduced with digital and analog clocks, ultimately supporting students to read hours and half hours. This unit extends that work, by fostering students' ability to prioritize chunks of five minutes to develop more facility with reading the minute hand on the analog clock. The prioritizing of fives is supported by building a connection to coins, in particular pennies, nickels, and dimes.

The teaching of time has often been misconstrued as the "telling of time." Being able to read and recite time from the face of the clock does not mean that children understand time, the passing of it, or the mathematics involved in the measuring or marking of it. This unit is part of a series that is crafted and sequenced carefully to foster those understandings.

The unit is designed to align with the CCSS Standards of Practice and the following core objectives:

Work with time and money.

CCSS.MATH.CONTENT.2.MD.C.7

Tell and write time from analog and digital clocks to the nearest five minutes, using a.m. and p.m.

CCSS.MATH.CONTENT.2.MD.C.8

Solve word problems involving dollar bills, quarters, dimes, nickels, and pennies, using $ and ¢ symbols appropriately. Example: If you have 2 dimes and 3 pennies, how many cents do you have?

The Mathematical Landscape

What are young children's conceptions of time and how do they experience it? According to Piaget (2007, originally published in 1970), up until around the ages of 7 or 8, children are unable to evaluate time durations accurately. His early studies showed that young children's time judgements were context-dependent and closely bound up with the situation within which time was experienced. For example, they confused the difficulty of a task (such as putting lead disks vs. wooden disks in a bin) with time duration. Although the durations were the same, children believed that it took them longer to do the heavy ones. Similar results were found by other researchers. When looking at a bright light versus a dim one (both on for the same duration), young children stated the bright light was on longer, evidence that they were confounding intensity of the light with time (Arlin 1989).

Current research, however, shows that the development of an understanding of time is much more complex than first thought. It turns out that even 6-month-old infants can discriminate two durations if the ratio of the durations is greater than a 2:1 (Brannon et al. 2007). Even younger infants with more limited capacities can discriminate different durations. During a training phase infants were presented with two sounds, one short (½ second) and one longer (1½ seconds). They were trained to look to the left after the short sound and to the right after the longer sound. In the later test phase, they were also presented with intermediate durations. The longer the sounds, the longer babies looked to the right (Provasi et al. 2010). In another study, children between the ages of 2-5 years were able to space their responses by a given time duration in order to make slides appear on a screen, and their ability to do so increased when they had to perform motor activities during the waiting period (Droit et al. 1990). Keeping children's attention focused on the passage of time raises their ability to discriminate and estimate durations. The higher the child's attention/concentration score, the better their sensitivity to time. This may explain why time duration estimation is often impaired in children with ADHD.

Time is continuous; it flows. And yet, humans over eons of years have found ways to mathematize it. We measure it in iterated chunks as if it weren't continuously flowing. We decompose our invented measurement chunks (like days) into hours, minutes, and seconds, and even into fractional units when we talk about half hours and half minutes. We interchange equivalent pieces, calling 30 minutes half an hour, or 1800 seconds; two-thirty is described as 2 hours and 30 minutes, as half-past two, and as 2½ hours. To make matters worse, as teachers we must ensure our young students can read, write, and understand both digital and analog mathematical representations of this continuous pure scientific phenomenon we call time, and do it with meaning!

Historically, time has been taught in our schools as a reading and drawing activity, rather than as a math activity. The focus has been on "telling time" (reading it off a clock) and rendering a given time with a drawing of the clock's hands. Reading hands on a clock makes little sense to a child who has yet to construct the meaning of the measurement units and the durations they represent. This is as non-sensical as trying to teach a child about number by engaging him in the reading and writing of numerals and disregarding an understanding of cardinality. To help children understand time as measured durations, teachers have often used calendar activities and the counting of days in school (celebrating the 100th day). These activities have little to no effect on developing an understanding of the measurement of time because the durations are not continuous, and they are too long and erratic in duration. A day in school to a young child is removed from the continuous flow of time and does not help children understand time measurement as a day is too long a period to focus and understand what is being measured. During the day there are too many distractions to get a sense of the duration of the day, and the lengths of children's days vary. Some days feel very long, and some are experienced as very short, depending on the activities being done. Some days are actually even half days—days with early dismissals. Yet, they are counted as a day in school.

The mathematics ideas and strategies we use to measure time should not be thought of as just a rote list of skills to explain and practice. Telling and writing time using analog and digital clocks is an outcome of a long progressive journey of development comprised of several big ideas, strategies, and models.

The unit *Time and Money* is a serious attempt to make use of the research on children's notions of time and the progressive development of an understanding of the mathematics involved in the measurement of time. Money (pennies, nickels, and dimes) is used as a context simultaneously to further support children's ability to unitize 5-minute chunks—a critical idea needed to flexibly tell time with the analog clock. As you work through this unit there are several big ideas, strategies, and models on the landscape to encourage and celebrate. Figure 1 depicts the landmarks of development that you will likely see your students developing as you progress through the unit. A description of each follows.

The fuller landscape of the measurement of time is provided on page 12 so that you can situate the development you will likely see with this unit, on the fuller journey your students will travel as they develop a deeper understanding in the years to come.

The Landscape of Learning

BIG IDEAS

- Durations of time can be measured
- To compare durations a standard unit is needed
- Grouping: larger units can encompass (and be decomposed into) smaller units
- Part/whole: durations can be added and subtracted
- Durations can be cut into equal (fractional) portions
- Unitizing and place value
- Groups can be regrouped

STRATEGIES

- Uses standard units
- Uses addition and decomposition to determine overall duration
- Uses subtraction to determine how much more time is needed
- Substitutes an equivalent expression
- Using the five-structure
- Skip counting
- Generalized use of a repertoire of strategies for addition and subtraction based on looking to the numbers first

MODELS

- Coin Model
- Number Line
- Double Number Line
- Digital Clock
- Analog Clock

Figure 1

BIG IDEAS

As young children explore the investigations within this unit, several big ideas arise. These include:

Durations of time can be measured

As children attempt to unite their understanding of number and their understanding of linear measurement to time, they often first employ their knowledge of cardinality to measure time: they count. They may also count faster at times and slower at other times and it may not at first matter to them that some words have more syllables and take longer to say.

To compare durations a standard unit is needed

When two people count at different speeds and some words take longer to say, different answers result, and these discrepant answers begin to create disequilibrium to an earlier scheme based on cardinality. This brings children to eventually construct the idea that it is important to measure time with constant intervals, which an external device, like a timer or a clock, can provide.

Grouping: larger units can encompass (and be decomposed into) smaller units

Grouping is an idea that is developed as an extension of the earlier idea of using standard units. Iterated smaller units (like seconds) can be grouped into minutes, which in turn can be grouped into hours. As children come to realize that if larger units are used the total number of units needed is smaller, they can more appropriately choose a unit to use to measure a duration. For example, short durations would be best to measure in seconds; and longer durations might be best measured in hours and minutes. Very long durations might be measured in days or years. With money, one dollar (or a coin) can be decomposed into smaller units. For example, a quarter can be decomposed into 5 nickels, or into 2 dimes and 5 pennies.

Part/whole: units can be added and subtracted

It is the integration of the smaller units with the whole into a part/whole structure that supports children to come to realize that lengths of time can be added and subtracted. Now they can add on and use several addition and subtraction strategies they may have developed. For example, now they can defend why the difference between two durations can be determined by adding on or subtracting.

Durations can be cut into equal (fractional) portions

Once grouping is constructed, decomposing is on the near horizon. It is not a large step to consider how, if time durations can be added and subtracted, a duration can also be decomposed into fractional pieces. As children work with clocks and are exposed to the turning of the hands around a circle, and as they explore cutting rectangles and circles into equal pieces, they develop an early understanding of halves and fourths. This allows them to consider how an hour can be cut into half hours or quarter hours. Children are also helped by their knowledge of cardinality, and in particular their knowledge of doubles. Understanding that 30 + 30 = 60, helps them come to understand that 30 minutes is equal to a half hour. As they get older they become more flexible in seeing 15 minutes as a quarter of an hour, or as 3 groups of five minutes.

Unitizing and place value

At first children may think that a timer should register 60 seconds (after 59 seconds) instead of a minute. They expect it should say 00:60 first and then go to 01:00 next, and they are quite surprised to see that the counter goes from 00:59 to 01:00. They understand that 60 seconds makes a minute; but, coming to deeply understand that one notation can be substituted for another is quite another story. It requires unitizing the 60 seconds into a new unit and shifting it a place! This is a huge cognitive leap akin to deeply understanding place value. The new value (1 minute) is represented in a new place, replacing 60 seconds.

Groups can be regrouped

Once unitizing is constructed, the door opens for groups to be regrouped into a variety of possibilities. For example, minutes can be grouped into groups of five, 2 groups of 5 minutes can be regrouped into 10 minutes, and 3 groups of 5 can be regrouped into 15 minutes, or ¼ of an hour. Coins can also be grouped and regrouped.

STRATEGIES

As you work with the activities in this unit, you will notice that students will use many strategies to solve the problems that are posed to them. Here are some strategies to notice:

Uses standard units

Once children construct the idea that the intervals of the count need to be regular, that pausing between counts and/or using longer words matter, they come to the realization that a standard unit is necessary for reliable measurement comparisons. When they learn of timers and clocks, they use them with meaning.

Uses addition and decomposition to determine overall duration

Whereas children determined length of time earlier by counting (or having the timer keep track of individual units), they now use addition. If an hour has passed and then 30 seconds more, they add the pieces saying it took one hour and 30 seconds, or 1 hour and a half.

Uses subtraction to determine how much more time is needed

Subtraction is used to calculate the measurement of missing pieces. For example, if a total duration is known (2 hours), as well as a given duration (1½ hours), subtraction (or adding on to find the missing addend) is used to determine the length of the missing unknown section. In later grades, this strategy develops into several flexible strategies for calculating elapsed time.

Substitutes an equivalent expression

An important algebraic strategy for measurement is when a child exchanges one numeric expression for an equivalent one. For example, a child might say 15 minutes is ¼ of an hour, or 60 seconds is a minute, knowing one equivalent expression can be exchanged for another.

Using the five-structure

As children work with the analog clock, they begin to note that the numbers not only represent the hours, the numbers also represent the unitizing of the groups of 5 minutes. Now they can use their prior knowledge of fives to read minutes in groups of five. The little hand refers to the 2 as 2 hours when it is pointing to it, but the big hand pointing to the 2 has a different meaning; it means 2 groups of 5, or 10 minutes past the hour. It is the underlying big idea of unitizing that opens the door for the use of the five-structure in flexible ways. The big hand pointing to the 5 means 25 minutes after the hour (5 groups of 5), but when it is pointing to the 7, it can mean 35 minutes after the hour (7 groups of 5), or 25 minutes of the hour (5 groups of 5 more to go). This is a hallmark strategy to support, and the previous development is required.

Skip counting

As children work with the five-structure they frequently skipcount saying, 5, 10, 15, 20. It is 20 minutes past 3. They also may use skip counting to determine how much more time is needed when comparing two durations. When counting coins, they skip count by the value of the coin.

Generalized use of a repertoire of strategies for addition and subtraction based on looking to the numbers first

Eventually students bring their full repertoire of addition and subtraction strategies based on a strong understanding of number and operation to any context, time or money. When determining elapsed time and calculating sums or differences they look to the numbers first and use a strategy to make the computation easier. Strategies like constant difference, compensation, use of doubles and near doubles, or regrouping are all used where appropriate.

MATHEMATICAL MODELING

Model of a situation

Initially models emerge as a representation *of* a situation; later they are used by teachers to represent children's computation strategies. Ultimately they are appropriated by children as powerful tools *for* thinking (Gravemeijer 1999). As you progress through this unit, your children will engage in determining the amount of money made over an hour, when a penny is earned for every minute. They will also need to determine the possible number of nickels, dimes, and quarters that can be exchanged for the pennies. The use of coins in a unit on time is purposeful as they support students to consider time in similar chunks: groups of five minutes (nickels); groups of ten minutes (dimes); and quarter hours (3 nickels, a dime and a nickel, or 15 pennies) and half hours (6 nickels, 3 dimes, or 30 pennies). The coins also support students to realize that hours are not equal to dollars as hours are equal to 60 minutes (60 pennies), and ¼ of an hour is only 15 cents, not a quarter. This recognition is critical so that in later years as students attempt to determine elapsed time using a regrouping procedure, they regroup with meaning using a whole of 60, not base ten.

Model of Student Strategies

Children benefit from seeing the teacher model their strategies on an open number line. Once the model has been introduced as a representation of the situation, for example as with the CFLM unit *Measuring for the Art Show,* you can use it to model children's addition and subtraction strategies as they work to determine differences in durations. The double number line model, where one expression is placed on the top of the line and another is placed underneath the line, is a great model to use to explore equivalence and non-equivalence of expressions.

Model as a Tool for Thinking

Eventually children take on the models as tools. They may solve elapsed time problems using an open number line or examine equivalence of amounts or durations using a double number line. They may image time on digital and analog clocks keeping track of hours and minutes. These are now used as tools for measuring time externally and serve as tools for thinking.

A graphic of the full landscape of learning for this unit is provided on page 12. The purpose of the graphic is to allow you to see the longer journey of students' development and to place your work with this unit within the scope of this long-term development. You may also find the graphic helpful as a way to record the progress of individual students for yourself. Each landmark can be shaded in as you find evidence in a student's work and in what the student says—evidence that a landmark strategy, big idea, or way of modeling has been constructed. Or, you may prefer to use our web-based app (www.NewPerspectivesOnAssessment.com) to document your children's growth digitally. In a sense, you will be recording the individual pathways your students take as they develop as young mathematicians.

References and Resources

Arlin, M. (1989). The effect of physical work, mental work, and quantity on children's time perception. *Perception and Psychophysics*, 45 (3) 209-214.

Beishuizen, Meindert (1993). Mental strategies and materials or models for addition and subtraction up to 100 in Dutch second grades. *Journal for Research in Mathematics Education,* 24, 294–323.

Brackbill, Yvonne and Hiram E. Fitzgerald (1972). Stereotype Temporal Conditioning in Infants. *Psychophysiology.* 9 (6), 569-577.

Brannon, E.M., Suand, S, and Libertus, K. (2007) Temporal discrimination increases in precision over development and parallels in the development of numerosity discrimination. *Developmental Science* 10, 6, 770-777.

Droit, S., Pouthas, V., and Jacquet, A.Y. (1990) Temporal learning in 4½ - 6-year-old children. *Journal of Experimental Child Psychology*. 50 , 305-321.

Gravemeijer, Koeno (1999). How emergent models may foster the constitution of formal mathematics. *Mathematical Thinking and Learning 1* (2): 155–77.

Hill, Fleet and George E. Forman (1984). *Constructive Play*. NY: Abel.

Klein, Anton S., Meindert Beishuizen, and Adri Treffers (2002). The empty number line in Dutch second grade, In *Lessons Learned from Research,* eds. Judith Sowder and Bonnie Schapelle. Reston, VA: NCTM.

Piaget, Jean (2007, original version 1970). *The Child's Conception of Time.* Oxfordshire, London: Routledge.

Provasi,J., Rattat, A.C. and Droit-Volet, S. (2010). Temporal bisection on 4-month-old infants. *Journal of Experimental Psychology: Animal Behavior Processes*. 37 (1), 108-113.

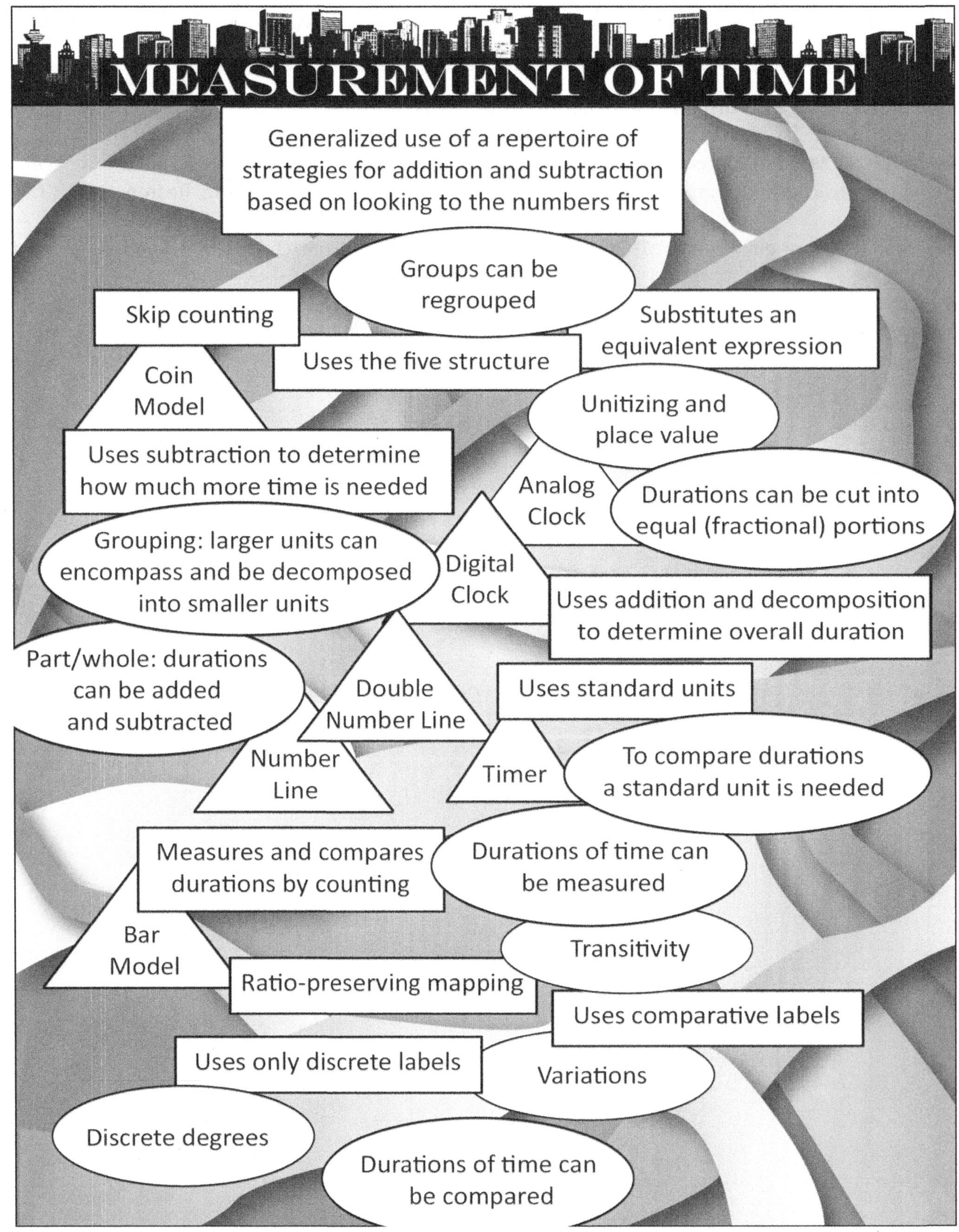

The Landscape of Learning: measurement of time on the horizon showing landmark strategies (rectangles), big ideas (ovals), and models (triangles)

DAY ONE

WHAT TIME IS IT?

Materials Needed

A class-size analog clock, preferably a MathRack® clock

Directions for playing the game *What Time is It?* (Appendix A)

Sets of Time Cards for playing the game *What Time is It?* (Appendix B, one set of cards per pair of students)

Sets of Clock Cards for playing the game *What Time is It?* (Appendix C, one set of cards per pair of students, **marked with hands to match the time cards before you make sets)**

Math Journals

Pencils

Today begins with a minilesson using analog clock images of hours and half hours, and then a matching game using cards with digital and analog clock faces is introduced. The game is the same game that was used at the end of the unit *The Timekeepers.* It is used here again to provide you with an opportunity to assess your students. If matching digital and analog clocks using hours and half hours is difficult for your children, you should start your work on time with the unit *The Timekeepers* and then continue with *Time and Money,* effectively making your work on time into a 10-day unit. If your students exhibit a strong understanding of hours and half hours in the minilesson and as they play *What Time Is It?* then just continue with this unit.

Day One Outline

Minilesson: a string of related problems

❖ Using the clock, work on a string of clock images comprised of hours and half hours, showing one image at a time and inviting discussion.

Developing the Context

❖ Introduce the game *What Time is It?* in a fishbowl with a student, modeling how to play, for the rest of the class to see.

❖ Pass out sets of cards to pairs.

Supporting the Investigation

❖ Note students' strategies as they work and encourage discussion on cards that can be matches.

❖ This is also a good time to assess, determining which students if any may need earlier work on time, specifically the work in *The Timekeeper* unit.

Minilesson: Clock Images

Show images on the analog clock (one-at-a-time) of the times listed below in the string, each time asking, *"What time is it?"* Invite discussion and once everyone agrees with the time write it in a digital version but also use the language in the string (for example writing and saying 12:30, but also saying half-past twelve). As you move from one image to another in the string, invite children to talk about what the hands have done. For example, to get to 12:30 from 12:00, the minute hand moved 30 minutes—half an hour more. As you work through the string, move the hands to represent what students say.

The String:

twelve o'clock (12:00)
half-past twelve (12:30)
one o'clock (1:00)
three o'clock (3:00)
half-past three (3:30)
half-past four (4:30)
half-past five (5:30)
six o'clock (6:00)

Behind the Numbers

The times have been chosen carefully to support students to consider, not just what the clock says, but also to consider the duration of the time change. The duration of elapsed time from 12:00 to 12:30 is 30 minutes, or half an hour. Providing the images consecutively supports students to understand why 12:30 can also be referred to as half-past twelve. By doing one o'clock next, students are challenged to consider how the other half an hour completes a full turn of the minute hand, but also why 1 o'clock comes next. This is an opportunity to explain that there are only 12 hours on a clock and that midnight is 12 AM and noon is 12 PM. Although military time is expressed as 13:00, it is not advisable to get into this with your students at this point as it will likely be confusing since 13 is not on the clock. The elapsed time between 1:00 and 3:00 is 2 hours and this provides students with a chance to see that only the hours changed. The next 3 images build hours onto the half hour, until the end of the string, when 30 minutes more are needed to get to 6:00. You may be wondering why discussions on elapsed time are suggested here. Telling time is a meaningless activity for students unless they understand what is being measured. An analogy would be asking students to say the number aloud when the numeral is shown, without having any idea of the quantity!

Developing the Context

Teacher Note:

Before you make copies of Appendix C, draw hands on the clocks to match the times on Appendix B!

Ask students to form a circle in the meeting area and choose a student to join you in the center to play *What Time is It?* Turn all time cards (Appendix B) face-down. Turn all clock cards (Appendix C, with the hands added) face-up and arrange them in 4 equal rows. Ask, "What time is it?" and invite your playing partner to choose a time card from the deck and say it aloud. You must now find a match from the clock cards that are displayed face-up. For example, if the time is 8:00, you must match it with an analog clock image of 8 o'clock. The match is placed to the side with the matched times showing face-up. Now your partner asks, "What time is it?" and you turn over a time card and say it aloud. Play continues until all matches have been made. Play is collaborative with a goal to make as many matches as possible, effectively using all cards on the table. There are 24 possible matches. Once all matches have been made, players work to arrange them in a sequence from 12:00 to 11:30.

Supporting the Investigation

Move around and confer as students play. Note if children are challenged by reading the face of the analog clock. If so, you will want to start your work on time using an earlier unit in the series, *The Timekeepers.* That unit is designed to foster an understanding of the measurement of time durations in general, and then to specifically work on the reading of time to the half hour. Both units are designed as 5-day units (in contrast to the usual 10-day units of CFLM) so that if needed you can put the two units together to make a 10-day unit. If most of your students do well with the activities on this first day, then you can just continue with this 5-day unit.

Reflections on the Day

Today, students either reviewed what they already knew about hours and half hours, or they were challenged, and you have had an opportunity to assess where they are on the landscape. This formative assessment opportunity is an important one and it should help you decide whether to carry on with this unit, or to use *The Timekeepers* first and then return to this unit, effectively making a 10-day unit. If you have decided to just carry on with this unit, tomorrow students will be introduced to a context where two girls become dogwalkers and earn coins for the time worked. The context is designed to support students to consider 5-minute chunks of time and to gain more facility with telling and recording time using an analog clock.

DAY TWO

THE DOGWALKERS

Materials Needed

The Dogwalkers (Appendix D)

Accounting Ledgers (Appendix E, one copy per student)

Small analog MathRack® clocks, with alternating groups of 5 red and 5 white beads to represent minutes (one per pair of students)

Math Journals

Pencils

Coins as needed

The day begins with the reading of a portion of the story *The Dogwalkers.* Students learn about a dogwalking job and how two friends do it together for three days, for an hour each day. On the first day they are each paid a penny a minute. On the second day, they are each paid a nickel for every 5 minutes, and on the third day they are each paid a dime for every 10 minutes. Working in pairs, students calculate how much money the girls will make and prepare a bill for Mrs. Smith.

Day Two Outline

Developing the Context

❖ Introduce the context by reading *The Dogwalkers* (Appendix D, up to page 39.)

❖ Form pairs of students and provide each with small MathRack® clocks, a copy of Appendix E, and their math journals and pencils. Send them off to determine how much money the girls will make over the three days, so they can prepare a bill for Mrs. Smith.

Supporting the Investigation

❖ As students work, move around and confer. Encourage them to consider how the coins are related to the clock.

Math Journals

❖ Provide time for students to reflect and articulate their learning from the day.

Developing the Context

Read the first part of the story *The Dogwalkers* (Appendix D), stopping at the mark on page 39. Display Appendix E, Accounting Ledgers, and form pairs asking each student in a pair to determine whether they will do a sheet for Tanisha, or a sheet for Tamika. Ensure that each pair has a "Tanisha" and a "Tamika" and then send them off to work with their journals, pencils, and coins to figure out how much they will each make.

> **Tech tip:**
>
> Colorful versions of the appendices for this unit that you can display as you read the story are available on www.NewPerspectivesOnline.net.
>
> An online search of "dogs" or "dogwalkers" will likely provide you with several images of dogs that you can use to develop the context as well, if you wish.

Supporting the Investigation

Let students get settled and ensure everyone understands the goal of the investigation. Then listen in on some conversations and confer. Here are some strategies and big ideas you are likely to see emerging:

- Counting by ones. Some students will count by ones all around the clock, taking a penny for each bead (disregarding the colors), and then will recount the pennies, recording 60¢. Note whether they realize that the total number of minutes in an hour is 60 by asking them how many minutes are in an hour. If they say 60, and then don't get 60 pennies because they made a mistake in counting, does this bother them? Do they understand 1-1 correspondence—that the number of pennies should be the same as the number of minutes? Ask if they should be the same. If they see that the answer should be 60, then celebrate that understanding and suggest they explain that on their poster. As they work on the nickels, support them to see how now it is 1 nickel for every 5 minutes and suggest that skip counting by fives might be faster than counting everything by ones.
- Some students may begin by using 1-1 correspondence immediately, knowing already that on the first day each girl will make 60¢. To figure out the nickels, they may then skip count by fives. Bring their attention to the colors on the clock and as they move the minute hand help them draw connections to how the numbers on the clock seem to be matching the number of nickels. Support them to wonder why this is and help them come to see how each group of five minutes is one group and thus one nickel. This is the big idea of unitizing (see page 8, Overview of the Unit).
- Note what students do to figure out the third day, specifically the number of dimes. Do they count all over again by ones, or do they realize that one dime is equal to two nickels? Support them to notice and to wonder about how the number of nickels is related to the number of dimes and why the number of dimes is half the number of nickels. Support a conversation on the equivalence: 60 pennies = 12 nickels = 6 dimes.
- Other students may work in half hour chunks because the context suggests doing 2 walks with the dogs—a half hour in the morning, and a half hour in the evening. Do they see that they can now double? If they add 30 + 30 for the pennies, do they see why that is 6 nickels + 6 nickels, and then

3 dimes + 3 dimes? Support a conversation on the equivalence and also help students notice how the 6 is at the half hour mark, and the 12 matches where the minute hand lands after one full rotation. Promote conversation on how the number of nickels matches the numbers on the clock. Connect what they are doing to the reading of the minute hand (5 after, 10 after, quarter after, etc.)

- You may also find several students who just add up the 3 hours: 60 + 60 + 60. If they add correctly, they will find that each girl will make $1.80 and the bill for Mrs. Smith should reflect this. This is a great strategy and it shows that the students understand the connection of the nickel to 5 minutes and the dime to ten minutes and that they know it is 60 minutes each day. As you confer, congratulate them on this, but also use the context of the coins and invite them to prove their thinking and to think about the number of each coin the girls would get. It's important that they also see the prioritizing of the chunks of 5 minutes on the clock.

Inside One Classroom: Conferring with Students at Work	
Juanita (the teacher): I'm so interested in the strategy that you are working on. May I sit and confer with you? It looks like you are skip counting by fives as you work on the nickels. Am I right? **Daniel:** (smiling) Yes. **Jessie**: We noticed the colors. It goes red, white... see? So that is 5, 10....like that.	 *Author's notes*
Juanita: Oh, what a good idea! That makes getting the minutes easy to count, doesn't it? Let's look at the minute hand of the clock as you do this and see what it does. When you say 5, where is the hand? **Daniel:** It's here on the 1, see....it passed all the reds. **Juanita:** Wow! And that is a nickel? What a great way to think about it! Hmm....did you notice how the number of nickels you are writing as you skip count matches these numbers on the clock? That's interesting, isn't it? I wonder why that is? **Jessie:** Oh yeah! Hey Daniel, I don't think we even have to keep going. It will be 6 nickels when we do 30 minutes, and then 12 nickels for the hour. Maybe the 1 means 1 group of 5, and then the 2 is 2 groups of 5.	*As Juanita confers, notice how she starts the conferral by listening and getting clarification and then she celebrates the approach. After clarifying and celebrating, she challenges by focusing attention on the numbers on the clock and the number of nickels.*
Juanita: What do you think, Daniel? Is Jessie right? Could the numbers be marking the minutes in groups of five, like the colors, so when I move the hand here it is 5 after the hour, then 10 after, then 15 after?	*Note how Juanita goes back and forth between the two students to ensure the conversation does not become a dialogue between her and one student. She engages both students in the conversation.*

Daniel: *(Pondering at first).* Oh yeah! And 15 is half of the 30. So, it is 3 nickels here and then 6 nickels there: red, white, red, white, red, white. **Juanita:** Hmmm....so you said 15 was half of the way to a half hour? What do you think, Jessie? **Jessie:** *(Pondering but then grinning).* Oh yeah! The line goes across the clock there and another line goes up and down here. **Juanita:** So how many chunks of 15 minutes are in an hour? This is one you said, ...where the 3 is? And the next chunk of 15 minutes gets you to the 6? Are there more? **Daniel:** Maybe here (pointing to the 8) ......no.......here (pointing to the 9). It has to be 3 numbers for 3 nickels. **Jessie:** Hey! 3, 6, 9, 12. That's 3 nickels, 3 nickels, 3 nickels, and 3 nickels. **Juanita:** I think I hear you saying something big here. Are you saying there are 4 equal sections in the hour that are 15 minutes each? So, if the hand moves to the 3 that is a quarter past the hour? And when it gets to the 6, that is half past? When the hand points to 9 how much more is needed?	. *Juanita asks a powerful question here. Her question is going to focus conversation on quarters of an hour.*
Jessie: 15 more minutes. See, 3 more chunks of 5 minutes. 5, 10, 15. **Juanita**: Oh, very interesting, Jessie. Let's look at the hands. (putting both hands back to the 12). Here is 12 o'clock, right? When the minute hand moves to the 3 that is a quarter past 12, and when it gets to 6 that is half past 12. When it gets to the 9 you said it had a quarter more (15 minutes) to go? So, could we read this as a quarter to 1? Lots to think about here! Why don't you make some notes in your journals about this to help you hold on to these ideas? This is big, and I would love you to talk about this in our congress tomorrow.	*Juanita connects what they are doing to the minute hand and then celebrates what the students have done. Then she leaves them to think. They have hit on something big. By going off she provides them with reflection time to write in their journals.*

Math Journals

During the last five minutes of class, ask students to write in their math journals about the big "a-ha" moments or discoveries they had today. Taking the time to reflect will help them hold on to their ideas, expose areas of confusion, and set the stage for tomorrow's work. Reading these entries tonight will help you, the teacher, see where each student is on the landscape of learning. Towards that aim, ask students,

"Before we end for today, write about your latest thinking using words and pictures of the clock so that you can hold on to your ideas and not forget them. Did you have a big idea today that you want to remember and write about tomorrow, or work further on? I will read what you write tonight and write back to you."

Reflections on the Day

Today, students worked to determine how much money the girls in the story—Tanisha and Tamika—will make over 3 days as they walk the dogs. Familiarity with 30 minutes as half and 15 minutes as quarters (don't confuse this with 3 nickels, it is ¼ of an hour, not ¼ of a dollar) will affect their developing sense of time and ways to measure it and talk about it. Note the many ideas and strategies you witnessed emerging today and think about the gallery walk and math congress that you will hold tomorrow. Which strategies and ideas will be powerful to discuss?

DAY THREE

TIME AND MONEY

Materials Needed

Students' work from Day Two

Lined sticky notes, several per student

The Dogwalkers (Appendix D)

Blank Clocks for use on posters (Appendix I), **scissors, and glue sticks**

Poster or drawing paper and markers

Small analog MathRack® clocks, with alternating groups of 5 red and 5 white beads to represent minutes (one per pair of students)

Math Journals and pencils

Coins as needed

Today begins with students reading their math journals and noting the comments and entries you made as you reflected on what they wrote at the end of math workshop yesterday. Peer groups of 4 students each provide for subsequent discussion and then students return to work to make a poster for a gallery walk and congress. The focus of the congress is on the connection of the nickels to the 5-minute chunks of time and how the number of dimes is half the number of nickels because each dime is worth 2 nickels. Connections are also made to the reading of the minute hand on the analog clock.

Day Three Outline

Math Journals

❖ Provide quiet time with math journals for students to read the comments they have received and to revisit their own reflections from the previous day.

❖ Form peer review groups of 4 students by putting two pairs from yesterday together. After discussion of strategies and the big ideas they are working on, have students add to their journals and use them to make posters for a gallery walk and congress.

Facilitating the Gallery Walk

❖ Confer with children as they put finishing touches to their posters, asking them to consider the most important things they want to tell their audience.

❖ Conduct a gallery walk to allow students time to reflect and comment on each other's posters.

Facilitating the Math Congress

❖ Convene students at the meeting area to discuss a few important ideas they noticed about measuring time and reading the analog clock.

Math Journals

Provide students with about 5 minutes to read over your responses to their journal entries from Day Two. Move around and help them read your comments as needed. Ask them to write back to you if they wish, as doing so sets the expectation that journal writing in math is important and should be taken seriously. Then form peer review groups (comprised of 2 pairs each) and provide discussion time on the strategies used and what students have noticed as they worked on the problem. This time will also prepare students to return to their work if they are not yet finished and to make a poster. As they finish discussing their ideas, pass out chart paper, markers, copies of Appendix I (*blank clocks without hands*), scissors, and glue sticks and invite students to work on posters for a gallery walk and congress.

Facilitating the Gallery Walk

As students work on posters, move around and confer, asking them to consider the most important things they want to tell their audience and reminding them that it is important to explain or show how their strategies are connected to the clock. Explain that the clock images on Appendix C can be cut out and used on posters if helpful. For example, the clock images might show how the groups of five minutes on the clock are connected to the nickels. Support the use of invented spelling, just as you do in writer's workshop.

After a sufficient amount of time, have students display their posters in the classroom for their peers to view. If students have used drawing paper, you can display the posters around the room or on tables. Posters might also be displayed on easels or taped to a whiteboard. Once all the groups have placed their posters up for display, explain to your students that during a gallery walk they will walk around and look at the other posters. They will have an important job: reading to try to understand what another group is showing on their poster. Explain to students that they will walk silently around reading the posters. As they walk around they should be thinking about questions like, "Do I understand this?" "Is this like what I did on my poster?" "Is this strategy like mine, or is it different ?" "Am I confused about a part?" and "Do I disagree?"

Provide students with lined post-it notes, large enough to invite writing. Using very small post-its often causes students to write very little because they can't fit their writing on them; the result is short notes like, "I agree," or "Nice job."

Have students walk around and read a few of the posters silently for 5-10 minutes. Tell them they do not have to read every poster. Make sure that every poster gets read by at least a few children and that every poster gets at least a few sticky notes.

After the gallery walk, you can invite the groups to go back to their posters to see what comments were left. By having this gallery walk, you are encouraging your students to reflect and comment on written and visual forms of mathematics—something professional mathematicians do! They are learning to write and read viable arguments, one of the CCSS Standards of Mathematical Practice.

During the gallery walk it's important that you make comments on posters as well, so that students see you as a member of the community who is really interested in their thinking. Look for moments and places where you can show your students that you are seriously trying to understand their thinking and remember, you are their mentor. Appreciate their good thinking, comment on interesting approaches, and suggest where more detail could be helpful to support understanding. Raise questions that might push for generalization or further insights. As you move around, look for big ideas and strategies from the landscape. This will help you to plan which pieces of work you will select for the congress, if you haven't done that already.

Facilitating the Math Congress

Review the posters and choose a few that you can use for a discussion. Choose samples that will deepen understanding and support growth along the landscape of learning described in the Overview. There is not necessarily one best plan for a congress. There are many different plans that might all be supportive of development. You'll want to focus the congress on the connection of the nickels to the 5-minute chunks of time and how the number of dimes is half the number of nickels because each dime is worth 2 nickels. Also, provide discussion on the reading of the minute hand on the analog clock, for example when the minute hand is on 1, it can be read as 5 after the hour, and when the hand is on the 3, it can be read as a quarter past the hour.

Inside One Classroom: A Portion of the Math Congress

Juanita (the teacher): Jessie and Daniel, yesterday when I conferred with you, you were having a great conversation about your discovery about the connection of the numbers on the clock with the coins. Come tell us about your big idea and how it helped you read the clock.

Jessie: Well, ...first we noticed the colors of the beads on the clock... so we skip counted by fives. Then we noticed our big idea! Every group of five minutes was a nickel! And, the numbers on the clock told us how many nickels!

Daniel: Right. See...when the minute hand moves to the 3, it will be 3 nickels and it is 5, 10, 15 minutes. You can see it on the clock we made. It is 2:15, or 15 minutes after 2.

Juanita: How many of you noticed like Jessie and Daniel that the numbers on the clock were the same as the number of nickels? (*Most hands go up*). Let's turn and talk with an elbow partner about this. Why do the numbers match? (*A real buzz starts. Juanita moves around and listens in on several conversations and then eventually resumes whole group discussion*). Did anyone have a helpful partner? Roberto?

Author's notes

Juanita chooses to start the congress with a discussion by Jessie and Daniel. A conversation like this will be beneficial for all and will bring up the idea of the relationship of the nickels to the numbers on the clock. It will help most of her students consider the importance of the five-minute chunks on the analog clock. She provides pair talk here to heighten reflection. Asking if anyone had a

Roberto: Jessie and Daniel convinced me. There are 5 red beads and that is 5 minutes. That's 1 group of 5 and that is 1 nickel. **Juanita:** Wow! Put your hand up if you understand what Roberto said. (*Several hands go up, but not all.*) Tammy, you look confused. Tell us what is bothering you. **Tammy:** I get the nickel part, but I'm confused because when the minute hand is on the 3, I see how that is 3 nickels, but Ben and I said that is a quarter. The clock has 4 equal parts, see (*she points to the lines).* 15 cents is not a quarter. A quarter is 25 cents, and that is ….. 5 nickels, …not 3 nickels. How can it be a quarter of an hour, and be only 3 nickels?	*helpful partner implicitly sends the message that pair talk needs to be accountable talk.*
Juanita: Oh wow! What a good question! Thanks for asking that. Let's all talk about what Tammy noticed. When the minute hand is on the 3; that is quarter past 2. Tammy says, "Why isn't it 25 cents?" That's a quarter, right? Turn back to a partner again and talk about this. (*After several minutes of pair talk, Juanita resumes whole group discussion.)* Tammy, what are you thinking now? It looks like you and your partner had an idea about this? **Tammy:** Yes! We figured it out! The quarter is a quarter of a dollar! On the clock 25 minutes would be the 5, the hand would be pointing to the 5, and that is 5 nickels. (*Several surprised ohs and ahs*).	*Juanita invites disequilibrium—a powerful inducer of cognitive reconstruction, which is needed to help students see what is happening.*
Juanita: Interesting! Who else noticed that? (*several hands go up*). Then why on the clock when the hand points to 3 do we say a quarter past? Did anyone figure out why? Anthony? **Anthony:** I think because it is a quarter of an hour and that is 15 minutes. 15 + 15 is 30, and 30 + 30 is 60. **Maia:** Oh, I get it! (*Several others comment, too)*	*Now the conversation is on a big idea. A quarter of an hour is not the same thing as a quarter of a dollar.*

Math Journals

At the end of the congress, provide everyone with some further reflective writing time. You might ask students to write about an idea or strategy they thought was particularly powerful or a new idea they are now thinking about. Giving students time to articulate their new understandings will also provide you with important information that you can use as formative assessment. Take the journals home again tonight and read over the entries. Comment on them. Dialoguing in journals can be very powerful to keep thinking going and it is a great way to do assessment and to integrate literacy work with mathematics. Take a pic of the entry as evidence of learning!

Reflections on the Day

Math workshop began today with students looking at the comments they received in their journals, considering the questions and challenges posed, and extending or explaining ideas. Students continued deepening their understanding in peer review groups and as they made posters. The congress helped to solidify and extend everyone's understanding of the measurement of time. Giving children time to review their ideas, to justify their thinking, to extend their thinking to other examples, and to learn from each other's work contributes to the development of these young mathematicians in powerful ways, and the classroom becomes a true mathematics and literacy laboratory.

DAY FOUR

MRS. SMITH PAYS THE BILL

Materials Needed

Math Journals

Pencils

Analog Clock
(preferably one class-size from www.Mathrack.com)

The Dogwalkers
(Appendix D)

Ways to Make 80¢
(Appendix F, 1 copy per pair of students)

Coins as needed
(pennies, dimes, nickels, and quarters)

Drawing paper and markers

Today begins with students reading the comments you left in their journals last night and writing a response. Then, in a minilesson using a string of related images, students practice reading the clock to the nearest 5 minutes. Afterwards they work in pairs on a new problem: Mrs. Smith pays the dog walking bill by giving each girl one dollar, but she also owes them each 80¢ more and so she will need to give them coins. What possibilities exist that would make 80¢?

Day Four Outline

Math Journals

❖ Pass out journals and allow students time to read over your comments.

❖ Facilitate a conversation on some of the big ideas about measuring time by prioritizing chunks of five that were addressed in the journals.

Minilesson: Clock Images

❖ Do a string of related clock images focused on reading time to the nearest 5 minutes on the analog clock.

❖ Using the digital clock, invite students to consider what it should say if it shows the same time. Display this on a digital clock, or just write it.

Developing the Context

❖ Read the remaining portion of The Dogwalkers (Appendix D)

❖ Display Appendix F and provide a brief discussion on what students think the possible combination of coins might be that would make 80¢.

Supporting the Investigation

❖ Confer with students as they work, encouraging the exchanging of equivalent coin amounts.

Math Journals

Start math workshop by passing out math journals and allowing students time to read through your comments. For those students who may be challenged with the reading of your notes, move around and help them. Then start a brief conversation on the prioritizing of chunks of five as a way to estimate time.

Minilesson: Clock Images

Ask students to share the approximate times they go to bed. They will likely say a time within the range of 7 to 9. Ask them if that time is in the morning or in the evening. This question should result in some chuckles as they all say, "Evening! Of course." Ask if there isn't that exact time in the morning as well and then explain that because there are duplicates, humans decided they should make a way to tell which is which so that when they told a friend a meeting time, the friend would know which time was meant. Ask students if they know what midnight and noon are. Some students may know they are both 12:00, but many will likely not know. Explain that when midnight occurs (when they are all hopefully asleep), this is really when the day begins even though the sun isn't up yet. This 12:00 is called 12:00 AM. Show the hands at midnight and then turning to 12:05 AM (and also say 5 minutes after midnight). Then keep moving the hands to show 1 AM, then 2 AM etc. until you pass 6 AM and 7 AM (at which point ask them if that is when they get up to get ready for school). Continue on until you come to 12 noon and explain that now it is 12 PM. Keep turning the hands hour by hour, emphasizing the use of PM (discussing their bedtimes as PM), until you get to midnight when it becomes AM again. Explain that time never stops; it just keeps going and that is why saying AM or PM is important.

Now display the time on the class-size analog clock using the string below, starting at 12 o'clock AM (midnight). These are NOT quick images. Keep the image visible. Do one image at-a-time and ask students to estimate the time to the nearest 5-minute chunk. Let them see you move the minute hand, so they can determine if it is AM or PM, each time asking, *"What time is it?"* Invite discussion and once consensus is reached say the words and then also write the digital time as shown in the string. The third problem will likely be challenging as the words "quarter *of* 3" are quite different than 2:45. Several other images also will likely be challenging, so ensure enough discussion.

The String:

midnight (12:00 A.M.)
half-past two (2:30 A.M.)
quarter of 3 (2:45 A.M.)
quarter of 7 (6:45 A.M.)
quarter after 10 (10:15 A.M.)
noon (12:00 P.M.)
25 minutes after 3 (3:25 P.M.)
25 minutes of 6 (5:35 P.M.)

Developing the Context

After the minilesson, read the remainder of *The Dogwalkers.* Pair students and send them off to consider a variety of ways to make 80 cents with quarters, nickels, dimes, and pennies. Encourage students to find as many different ways as they can.

Supporting the Investigation

Provide coins if needed. Some students may not need them and will be able to work mentally; others may need them. As you move around and confer, note the strategies students are using and confer in developmentally-appropriate ways. Here are some tips:

- Some students will randomly choose coins and just add the amounts up without considering the values beforehand. For example, they might start by just doing random amounts of pennies, nickels, dimes, and quarters. If they end up with less than 80 cents, rather than adding more money (adjusting accordingly), they start a new randomly chosen amount. When you see this, encourage students to stop before they take a new amount and ask them if they need more money, or if they have too much. Encourage them to adjust the amounts accordingly rather than to just keep working with trial and error.
- Some students may try a variety of pennies and add by counting on. Ask them to think about what number of pennies might work (besides the 80). If they don't realize a multiple of 5 is needed (because the other coins can't be added to get to an even 80 otherwise), allow them to try a few combinations and realize they aren't working, and then support them to try exchanging some pennies for some nickels, pennies for dimes, and pennies for quarters. Help them notice how they are always removing chunks of fives.
- Some students may start with 3 quarters and a nickel. Compliment them on a great way to start as it is a way with very few coins and might therefore be the way Mrs. Smith decides to do it! Ask students what they are going to try next and encourage them to consider exchanging coins for equivalent amounts, for example what if Mrs. Smith doesn't have enough quarters? Might she exchange one of the quarters for 2 dimes and a nickel? What else could a quarter be exchanged for? Could the dimes be exchanged for nickels?

Teacher Note:

It is not expected in this investigation that students find all the possibilities. Because of the many ways multiples of 5 pennies can be exchanged for nickels, dimes, and quarters, there are a lot of possibilities. Just encourage students to consider possible exchanges. Focus on how one amount can be exchanged for an equivalent amount, for example how 2 nickels can be exchanged for a dime or how 5 nickels can be exchanged for a quarter. From earlier work with 5 and 10 minutes on the clock, they may see that since 80 cents can be made with 8 dimes, it can also be made with 16 nickels, and every nickel could be exchanged for 5 cents. It is the exchanging of equivalent values that is the focus.

Math Journals

During the last five minutes of class, ask students to write in their math journals about the big "a-ha" moments or discoveries they had today. Taking the time to reflect will help them hold on to their ideas, expose areas of confusion, and set the stage for tomorrow's work. Towards that aim, ask students,

> *"Before we end for today, write about your latest thinking, maybe a strategy you found helpful, or a big idea you are working on. Did you notice something really interesting today that you want to remember and write about tomorrow, or work further on?"*

Reflections on the Day

Today your students had the opportunity to further deepen their understanding of time and money. In the minilesson they learned about the use of AM and PM and worked on reading time on an analog clock to the nearest 5 minutes. In the subsequent investigation they explored a variety of ways to use pennies, nickels, dimes, and quarters to make 80 cents.

This unit is a short one, and several of your children may still be challenged with telling time to the nearest 5 minutes, or with identifying coins and their values and exchanging them for other equivalent amounts. Tomorrow they will have time to explore the coins further, and then they will have an opportunity for more experiences with telling time to the nearest five minutes with an extension of the game they played on Day One, but with a new set of cards.

DAY FIVE

WHAT TIME IS IT?

Materials Needed

A class-size analog clock

Sets of Time Cards for playing the game *What Time is It?* (Appendix G, one set of cards per pair of students)

Sets of Clock Cards for playing the game *What Time is It?* (Appendix H, one set of cards per pair of students *with hands added to match the new time cards*)

Sample student work from each activity in the unit

Chart Paper for the Learning Scroll

Markers

Glue sticks

Math Journals

Today begins with looking over journal notes and finishing up the work of yesterday. A short congress is then held on some of the possible ways to make 80 cents, with a particular focus on exchanging equivalent amounts. An extension of the game played on Day One *What Time Is It?* is then used but with a new set of cards to provide a further challenge with reading the clock to the nearest five minutes. Math workshop ends with the making of a learning scroll—a documentation of the learning and the activities that occurred over the duration of the unit.

Day Five Outline

Facilitating the Math Congress

❖ Convene students at the meeting area to discuss a few important ideas they noticed about the ways Mrs. Smith could use the coins to make 80 cents. Focus conversation on how equivalent amounts can be exchanged.

Developing the Context

❖ Introduce the game *What Time is It?* by modeling with a student how to play in a fishbowl for the rest of the class to see and reminding them that they played a version of it already on Day One of the unit.
❖ Explain that this version is a bigger challenge because since they now know more about time, you have some new cards.
❖ Pass out the new sets of cards to pairs.

Supporting the Investigation

❖ Note students' strategies as they work and encourage discussion on cards that can be matches. This is also a good time to assess.

Building a Learning Scroll

❖ Use children's ideas and samples of their work from throughout the five days of this unit to make a learning scroll of the progression of their thinking about time and money and display it.

Facilitating the Congress

Start the day with letting students review their journals and work further on the investigation from yesterday. Then bring students to the meeting area for a brief congress to share some of the strategies they found helpful and some of the combinations they found that worked. Focus the congress primarily on the idea of how equivalent values can be exchanged to find new possibilities.

Developing the Context

> **Teacher Note:**
>
> Before you make copies of Appendix H, make one copy and draw hands on the clocks to match the new times on Appendix G! Use this to make your new clock card sets.

Ask students to form a circle and explain that you have a new version of *What Time is It?* To remind everyone how to play, choose a student to join you in the center. Explain that you have new sets of cards to make the game more of a challenge now that they have learned a lot of new things about telling time. Turn all time cards (Appendix G) face-down. Turn all clock cards (Appendix H) face-up and arrange them in 4 equal rows. Ask, "What time is it?" and invite your playing partner to choose a time card and say it aloud. You must now find a match from the clock cards that are displayed face-up. For example, if the time is 8:05 PM, you must match it with an analog clock image of 5 minutes past 8. The match is placed to the side with the matched times showing face-up. Now your partner asks, "What time is it?" and you turn over a time card and say it aloud. Play continues until all matches have been made. Play is collaborative with a goal to make as many matches as possible, effectively using all cards on the table. There are 24 possible matches. Once all matches have been made, players work to arrange them in a sequence from 12:00 AM to 11:30 PM.

Supporting the Investigation

Move around and confer as students play. Note the developing flexibility to read the face of the analog clock to the nearest 5 minutes. This is also an opportune time to do some formative assessment. If you find some of your children are still quite challenged trying to read the clock face, make a note so that you provide them with more experiences playing the game post the completion of the unit.

Building a Learning Scroll

A learning scroll is a class display—a sort of " socio-historical" wall—documenting the progression of the unit, children's questions, the important ideas constructed over the duration of the unit, samples of students' work, and descriptions of their strategies and ideas, including anecdotes of how students' thinking changed over time. It is a document of the progression and emergence of learning over the past five days. By making this display available for some time, you allow your students to revisit and reflect on all the wonderful ideas and strategies that emerged as they worked throughout the unit and you also provide a look at an even longer time duration—one measured not in hours, but in 5 days (or 10, if you also made use of *The Timekeepers*).

Use a roll of chart paper and cut out a long length sufficient to cover a bulletin board or a display area in a hallway. Curl and staple the two ends, making a small roll on each end. Staple or tape it to the area to be covered. On the left begin with a short description of the first activity with a few samples of children's early work and ideas. Some teachers use pictures of the children and cartoon bubbles with quotes of some of the early ideas they had. Selectively pick key pieces of children's work from the five days of the unit (or take pictures of some pages of their journals with their permission) and include brief anecdotal descriptions of their ideas as they worked on activities. Provide documentation of the emerging learning with the pieces you pick. Wherever you can, show the developmental emergence of ideas from the landscape in the Overview. Display the scroll and ask children to look at it and reflect with you on all the wonderful ideas they constructed over the course of this unit. Keep it displayed for several weeks so that they can revisit again and again the notion of time as a measured duration in minutes (prioritizing the fives) and hours.

Reflections on the Unit

Absolute, true, and mathematical time, in and of itself and of its own nature, without reference to anything external, flows uniformly and by another name is called duration. Relative, apparent, and common time is any sensible and external measure (precise or imprecise) of duration by means of motion; such as a measure—for example, an hour, a day, a month, a year—is commonly used instead of true time.

Sir Isaac Newton

In this unit, your children had opportunities to extend their understanding of time as short durations to longer durations measured by hours, minutes, and days. The context of money along with the MathRack® clock also helped them prioritize 5-minute sections. As they worked with money, the coins were also examined as equivalent amounts that could be exchanged. Emphasis was placed on treating numeric expressions as objects: 2 dimes and 1 nickel could be exchanged for 1 quarter.

The focus of this unit has been not just on the "telling of time" but on the development of an *understanding* of time and the many ways to measure it and represent it. And now, most likely, you are witnessing several of your children using equivalent portions, unitizing them, and substituting and exchanging different representations with meaning, for example calling 1:45, a quarter to 2, one forty-five, 1 hour and 45 minutes, and even questioning whether it is in the AM or the PM.

Others may still be challenged. This is to be expected; this unit was a short one. It ended however with a game that you can use over and over throughout the year. You can also do minilessons with clock images with small groups for further support. Development takes time. Journey with your children, supporting their steps along the way with patience. Children, when they are respected as young mathematicians at work, come to see beauty all around them as they mathematize their lived worlds with mathematical creations based on their own meaning-making.

Appendix A—Directions for Playing *What Time is It?*

Set-up: All 24 time cards are shuffled and placed in a face-down pile in the center of the playing area. Make one copy of the clock cards and draw in hands to match each of the time cards. Then make copies of this page for each set. All 24 clock cards are placed face-up in 4 equal rows with the hands showing.

Game Play:

- Player One asks, "What time is it?" thereby inviting the playing partner (Player Two) to choose a time card and say it aloud.
- Player One must now find a match from the clock cards that are displayed face-up. For example, if the time card is 8:00, it is matched with an analog clock image of 8 o'clock. The match is placed to the side with the matched cards showing face-up.
- Turns alternate, so now Player Two asks, "What time is it?" and Player One turns over a time card and says it aloud. Player Two finds a matching clock card.
- Play continues until all matches have been made.
- Play is collaborative with players helping each other as needed. The goal is to make as many matches as possible, effectively using all cards on the table. There are 24 possible matches. Players use small individual clocks to help them.
- Once all matches have been made, players work to arrange them in a sequence from 12:00 to 11:30.

Appendix B—Time Cards for Playing *What Time is It?*

12:00	12:30	1:00	1:30
2:00	2:30	3:00	3:30
4:00	4:30	5:00	5:30
6:00	6:30	7:00	7:30
8:00	8:30	9:00	9:30
10:00	10:30	11:00	11:30

Appendix C—Clock Cards for Playing *What Time is It?* (1 of 4) [Make one copy first and draw hands in to match time cards. Copy that for sets of cards]

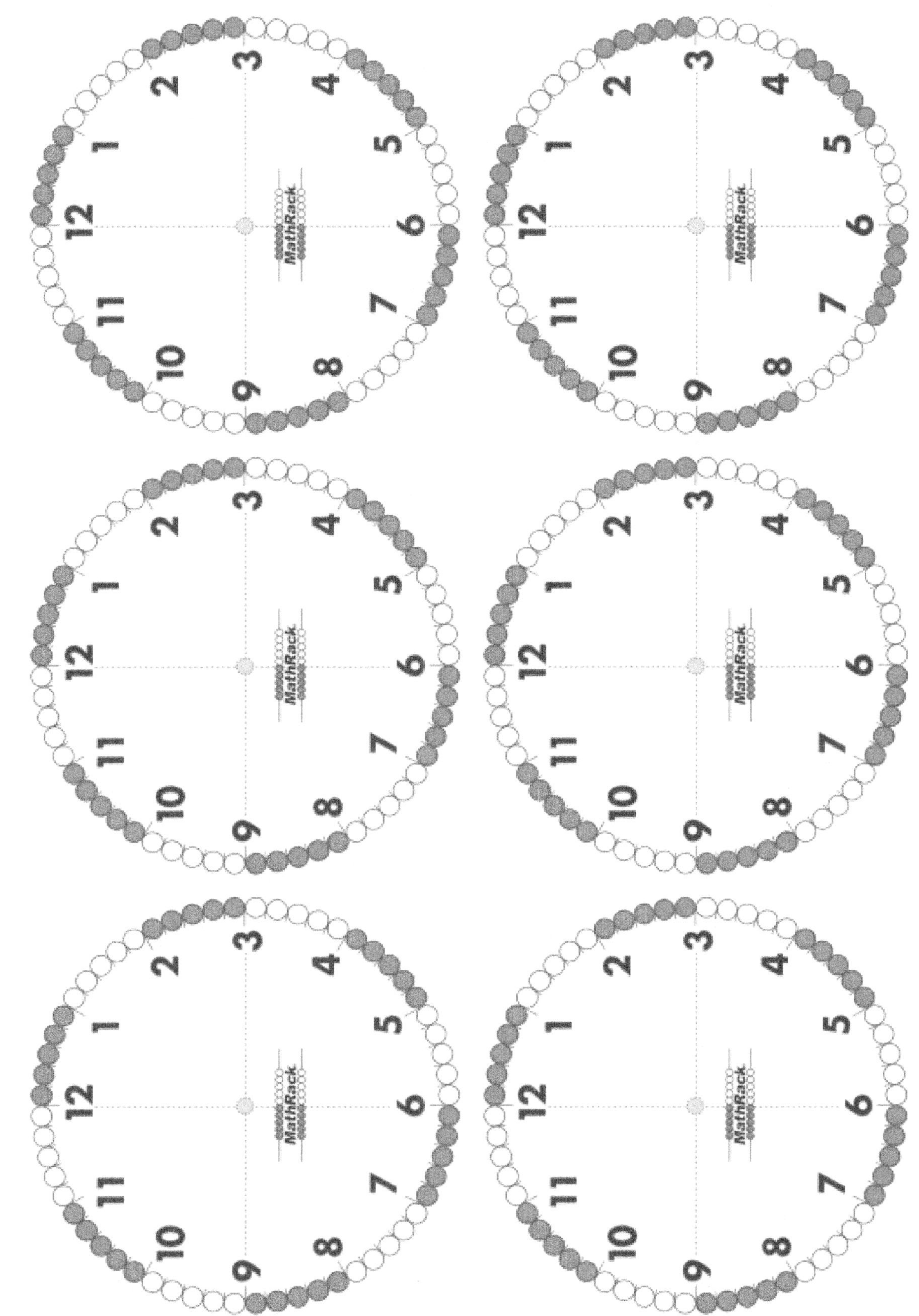

Appendix C—Clock Cards for Playing *What Time is It?* (2 of 4)

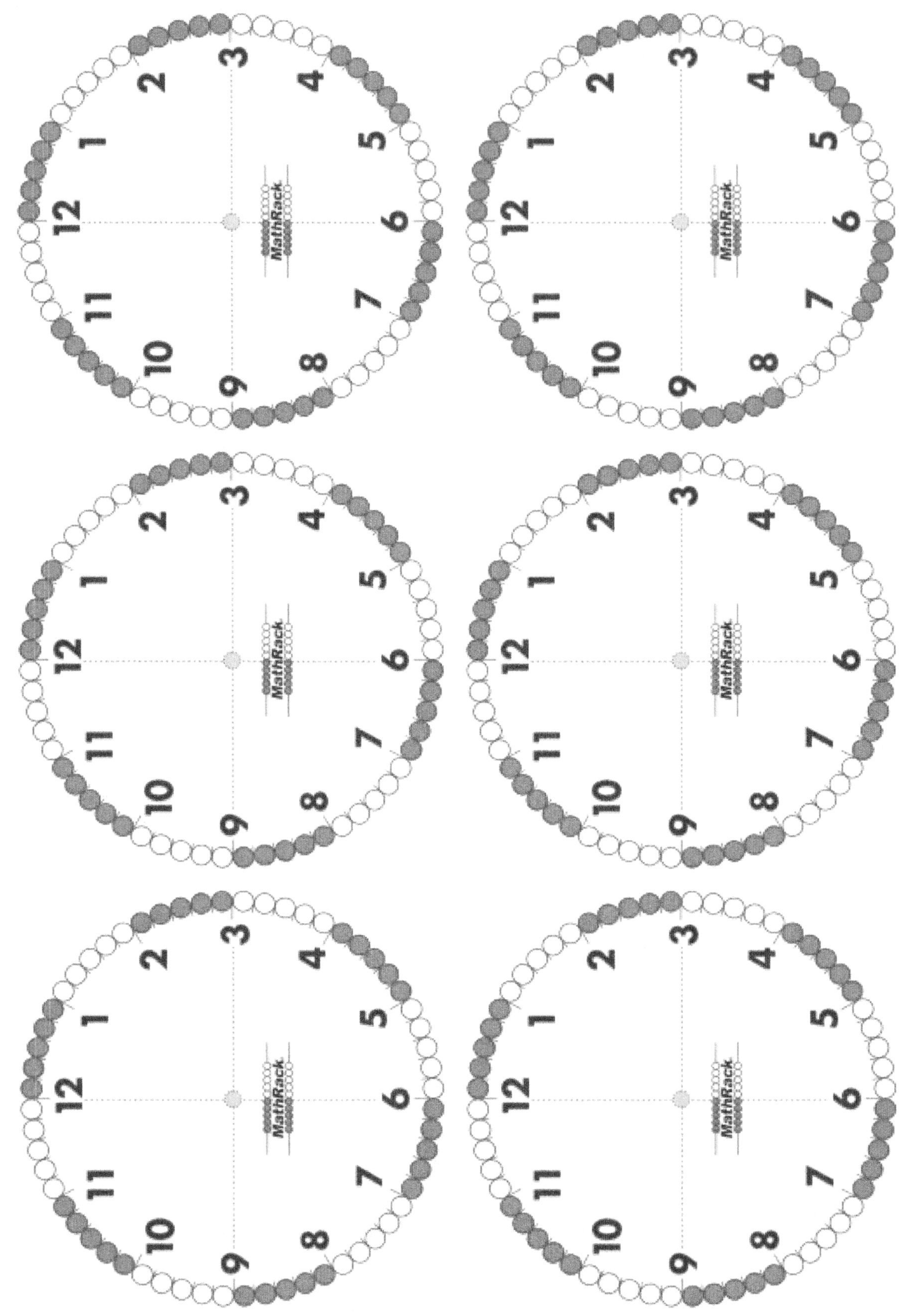

Appendix C—Clock Cards for Playing *What Time is It?* (3 of 4)

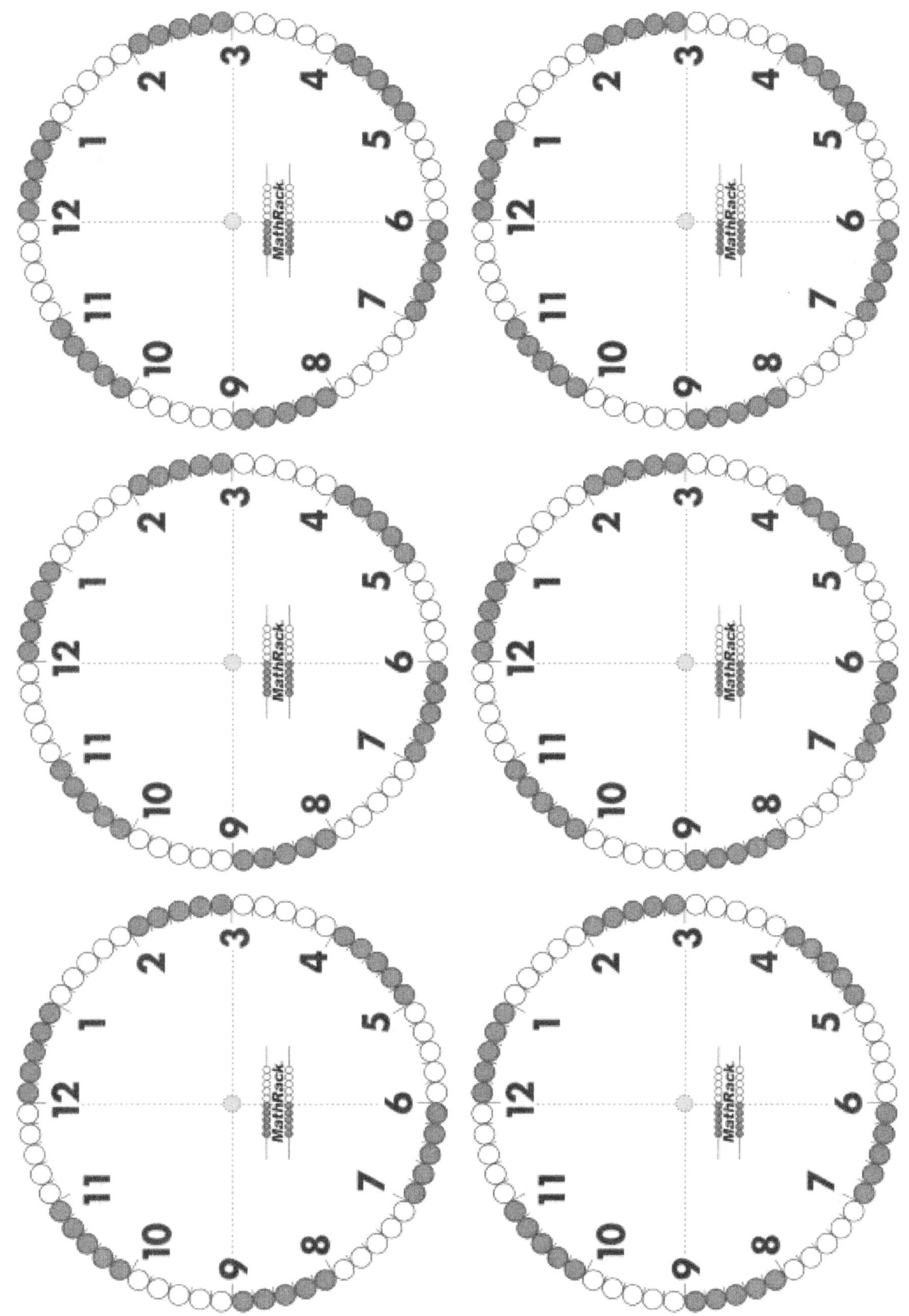

Appendix C—Clock Cards for Playing *What Time is It?* (4 of 4)

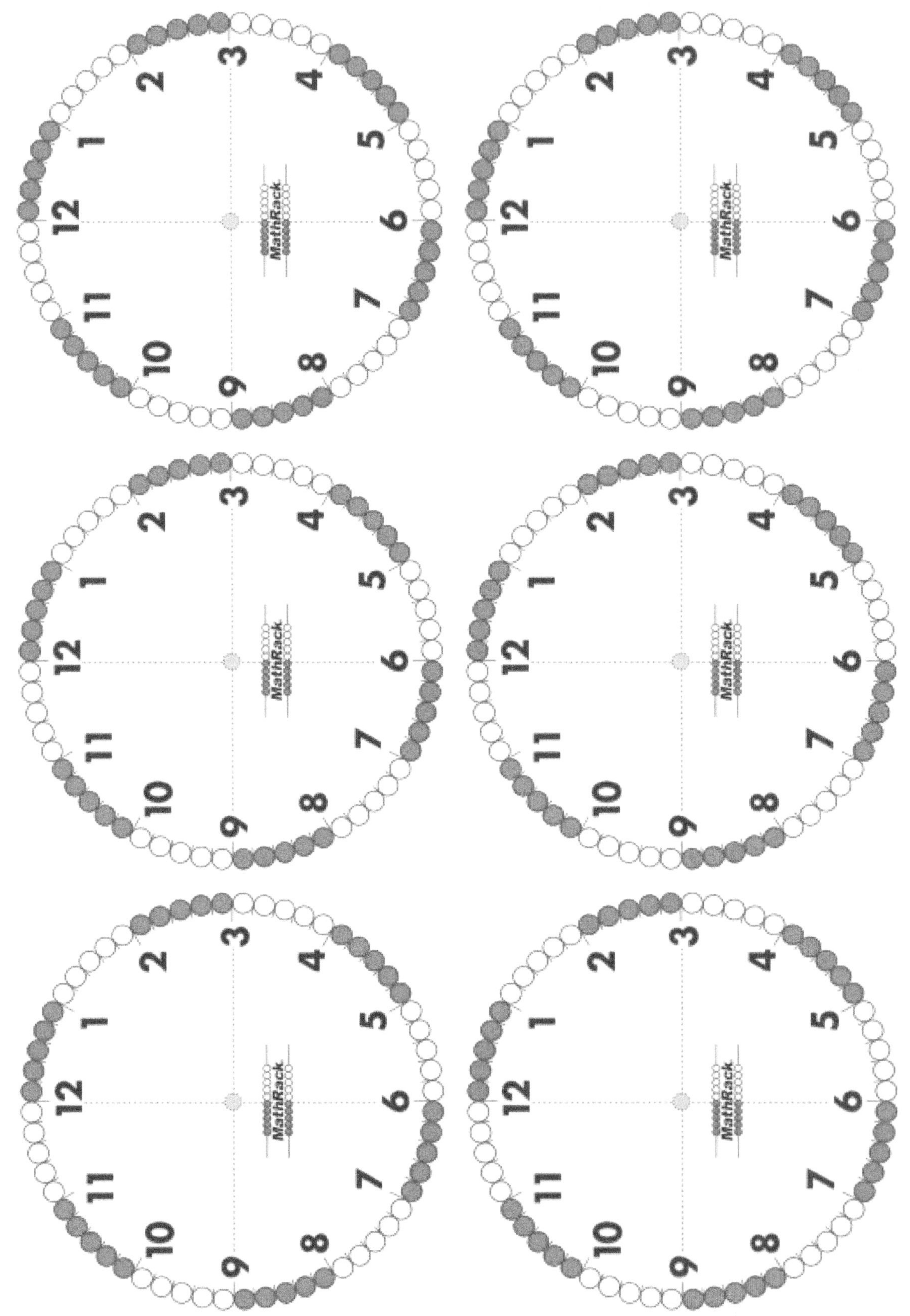

Appendix D—The Dogwalkers

Tanisha Arnold and Tamika Smith are best friends. They live next door to each other and have played together ever since they were little. Their birthdays are even just a few days apart and they are in the same grade in school!

The Smiths and Arnolds are very close families and often they help each other out when needed, like when one has to work late, or another has obligations that need attending to.

One day, Tamika's mom, Celeste, announced that she was going to need to be a way for a few days on a business trip.

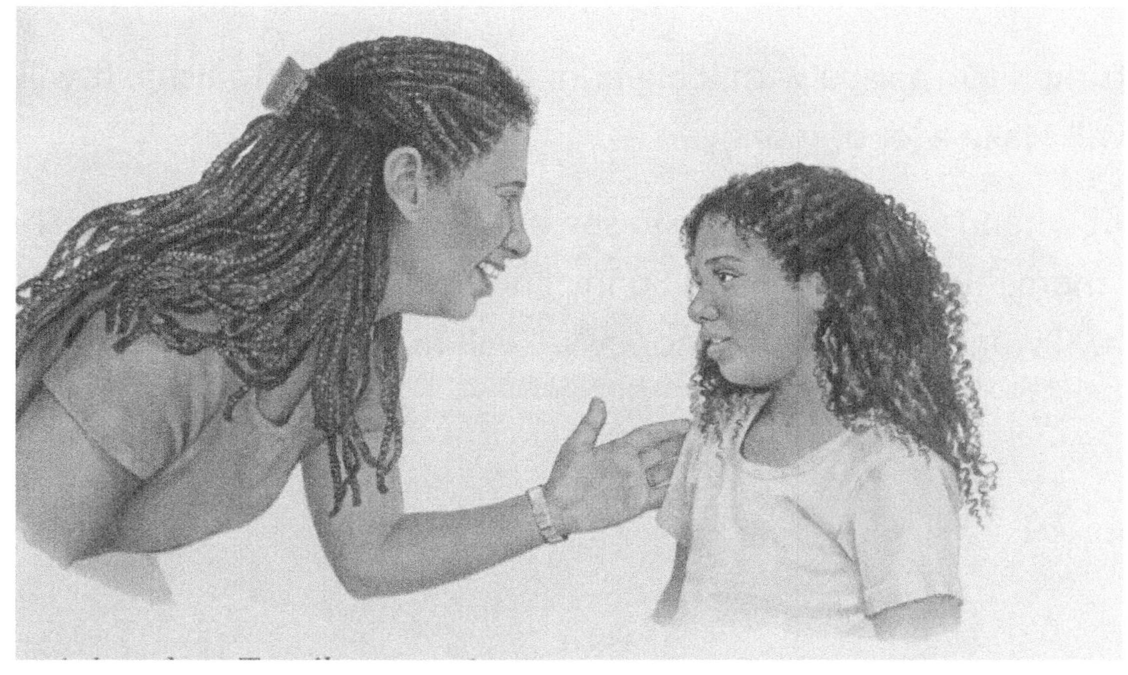

The Arnolds said, “No problem, Celeste, Tamika can stay with us.”

“Whoopie!” shrieked Tanisha. “A sleepover, and on school nights—not even a weekend!”

“We need to figure something out for Sunny and Bo, though.” Mr. Arnold said. Sunny and Bo were Tamika’s two dogs and if Tamika’s mom was away someone was going to need to walk them.

“I know, and I don’t like being away like this… but time is money, right? I do have an idea though,” Celeste said looking at Tamika and Tanisha. How about if I pay the two of you to walk the dogs for an hour each day. You can do a half hour in the morning and a half hour later in the day when you get home from school. You can each take a dog on a leash. Tamika knows how to do it because she often does it with me, right Tamika?”

“How much will you pay us?” both girls asked wide-eyed with excitement.

Mrs. Smith thought quietly for a minute and then she said, “Well, I’m going to be gone for three days. I’ll pay you each a penny a minute on the first day; a nickel each for every five minutes on the second day; and a dime each for every ten minutes on the third day.”

Tamika turned to Tanisha with a big grin. “We can do it, Tanisha. It will be fun, and we will make a lot of money.”

That night when Tamika went to bed she had a big smile on her face. She would miss her mom, but, taking care of Sunny and Bo with Tanisha was going to be a lot of fun. “I wonder how much money we will make?” she wondered.

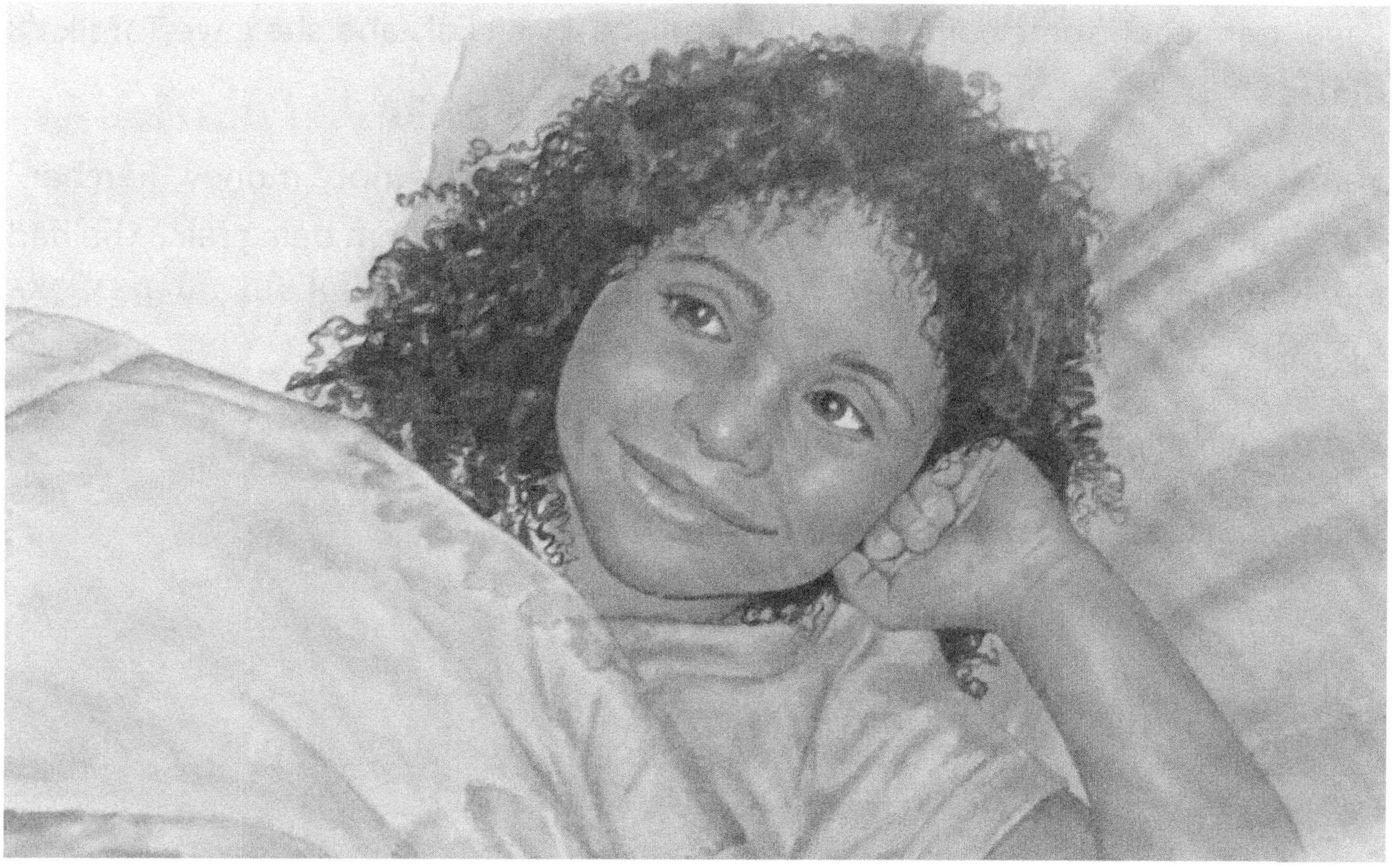

and begin the investigation on Day 1

Part Two: Start Here for the Investigation on Day Four.

When Mrs. Smith returned from her trip Tamika and Tanisha gave her their bills. On the bills they had each written, "You owe me 60 cents for the first day; 12 nickels for the second day; and 6 dimes for the third day." Underneath they had each totaled the amounts and had written: 60¢ + 60¢ + 60¢ = 180¢

Mrs. Smith said, "That's exactly what I figured on. Great job, girls! The dogs seem content, and I'm happy to pay you. 180 cents is the same as $1.80 because a dollar is the same as 100 cents, so here is a dollar for each of you." Then she gave them each some coins. She gave Tanisha 16 nickels and she gave Tamika 8 dimes.

Tamika felt like crying. Why was her mom giving Tanisha more money than her? They had both worked equally hard, so why wasn't her mom being fair? She had given Tanisha lots more coins—twice as many in fact—and they were even bigger!

Did the girls get the same amount of money?

What coins can be used to make 80 cents?

and begin the investigation on Day Four

Appendix E—Accounting Ledgers (1 of 2)

Tamika

Day One, a penny a minute (1¢ a minute)

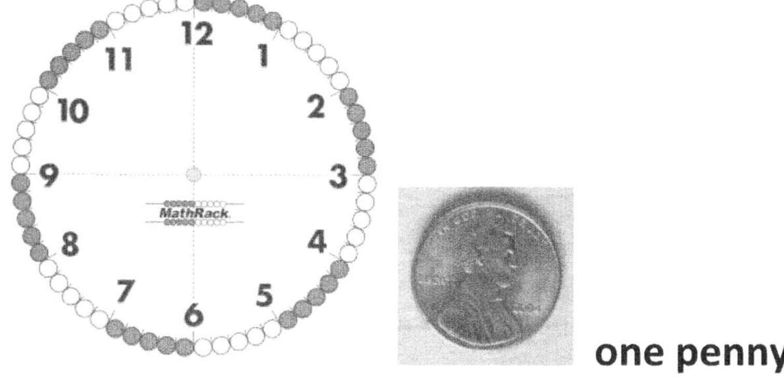

one penny

Day Two, a nickel for every five minutes (5¢ for 5 minutes)

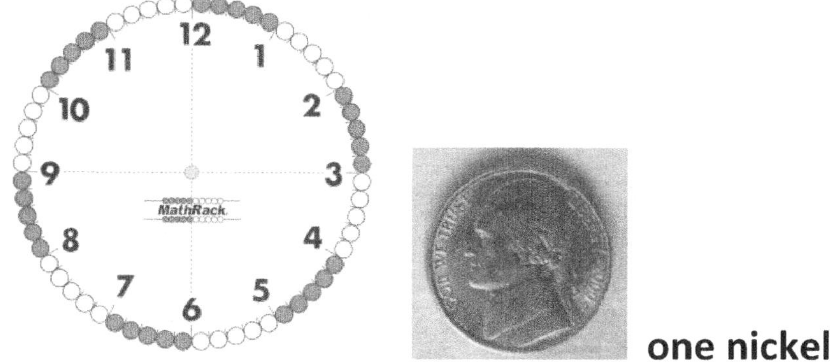

one nickel

Day Three, a dime for every ten minutes

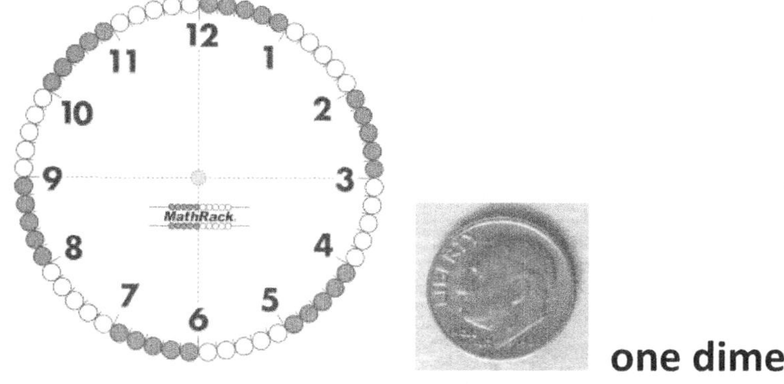

one dime

Appendix E—Accounting Ledgers (2 of 2)

Tanisha

Day One, a penny a minute (1¢ a minute)

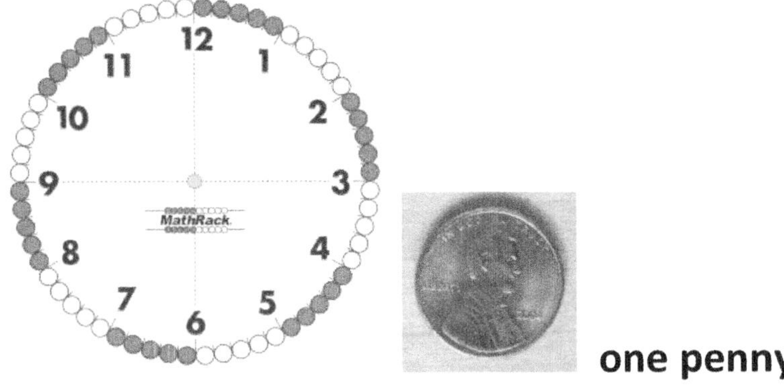

one penny

Day Two, a nickel for every five minutes (5¢ for 5 minutes)

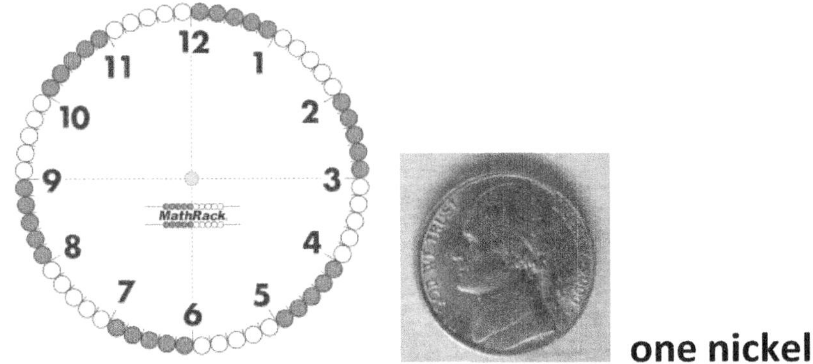

one nickel

Day Three, a dime for every ten minutes (10¢ for 10 minutes)

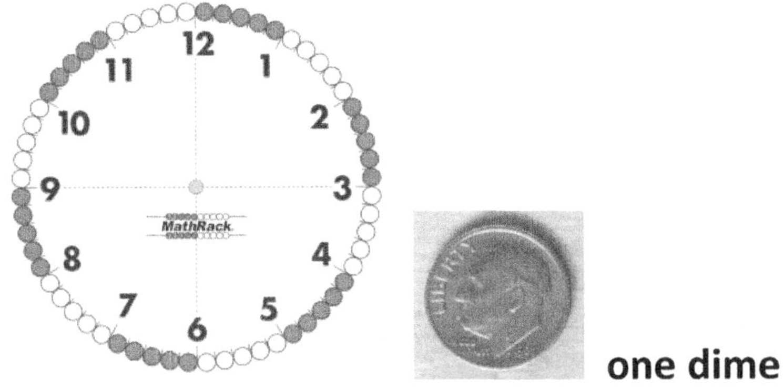

one dime

Appendix F—Ways to make 80¢

Pennies	Nickels	Dimes	Quarters
80			

Appendix G—Time Cards for Playing *What Time is It?*

12:00 AM	12:15 AM	1:45 PM	7:30 AM
2:10 PM	2:30 AM	3:15 PM	3:20 PM
4:00 AM	4:35 AM	4:35 PM	5:40 PM
6:00 AM	6:55 AM	7:00 AM	7:30 PM
8:00 PM	8:05 PM	9:00 AM	9:20 AM
10:00 AM	10:30 AM	11:05 PM	11:50 PM

Appendix H—Clock Cards for Playing *What Time is It?* (1 of 4) [Make one copy first and draw hands in to match time cards. Copy that for sets of cards]

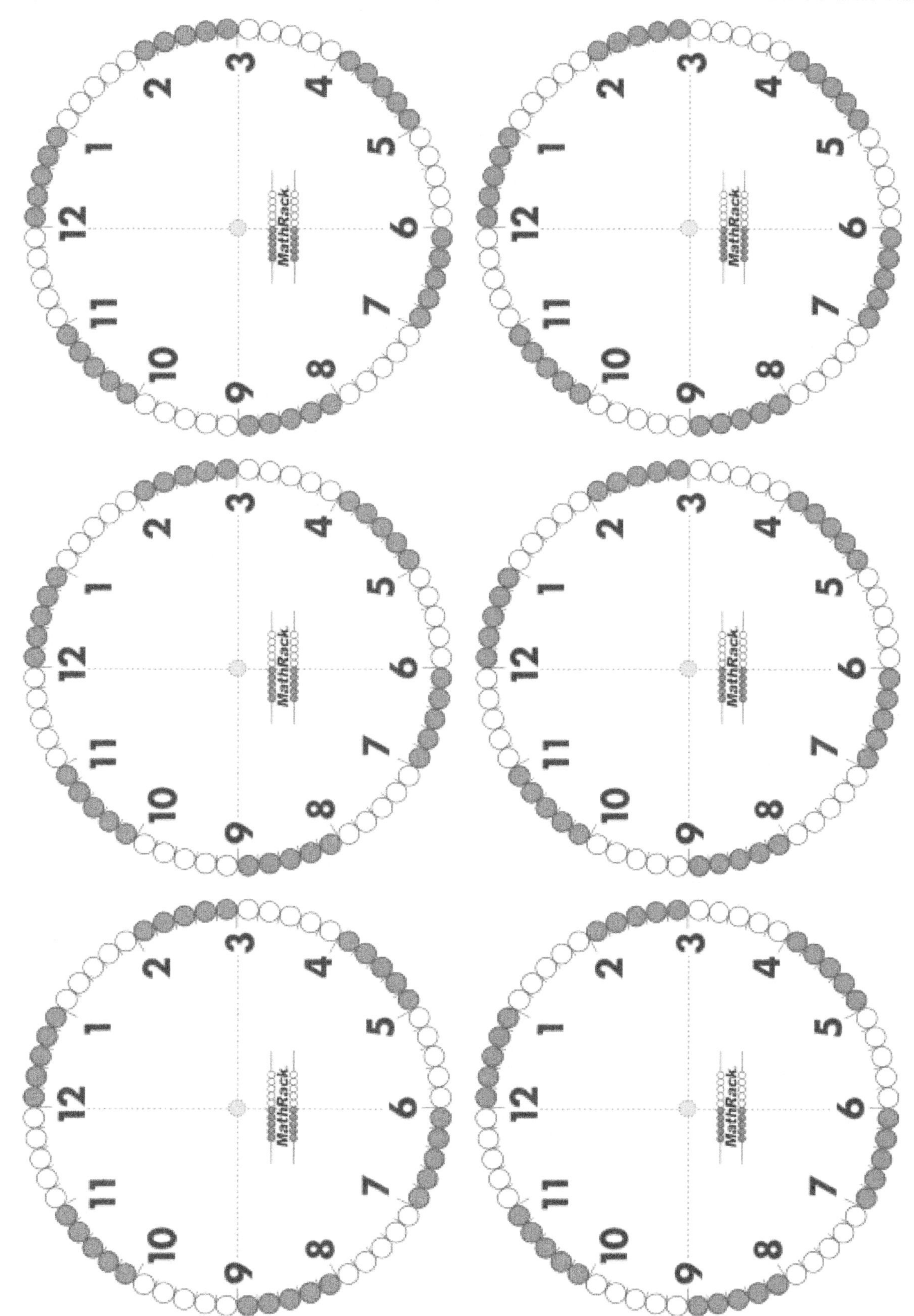

Appendix H—Clock Cards for Playing *What Time is It?* (2 of 4)

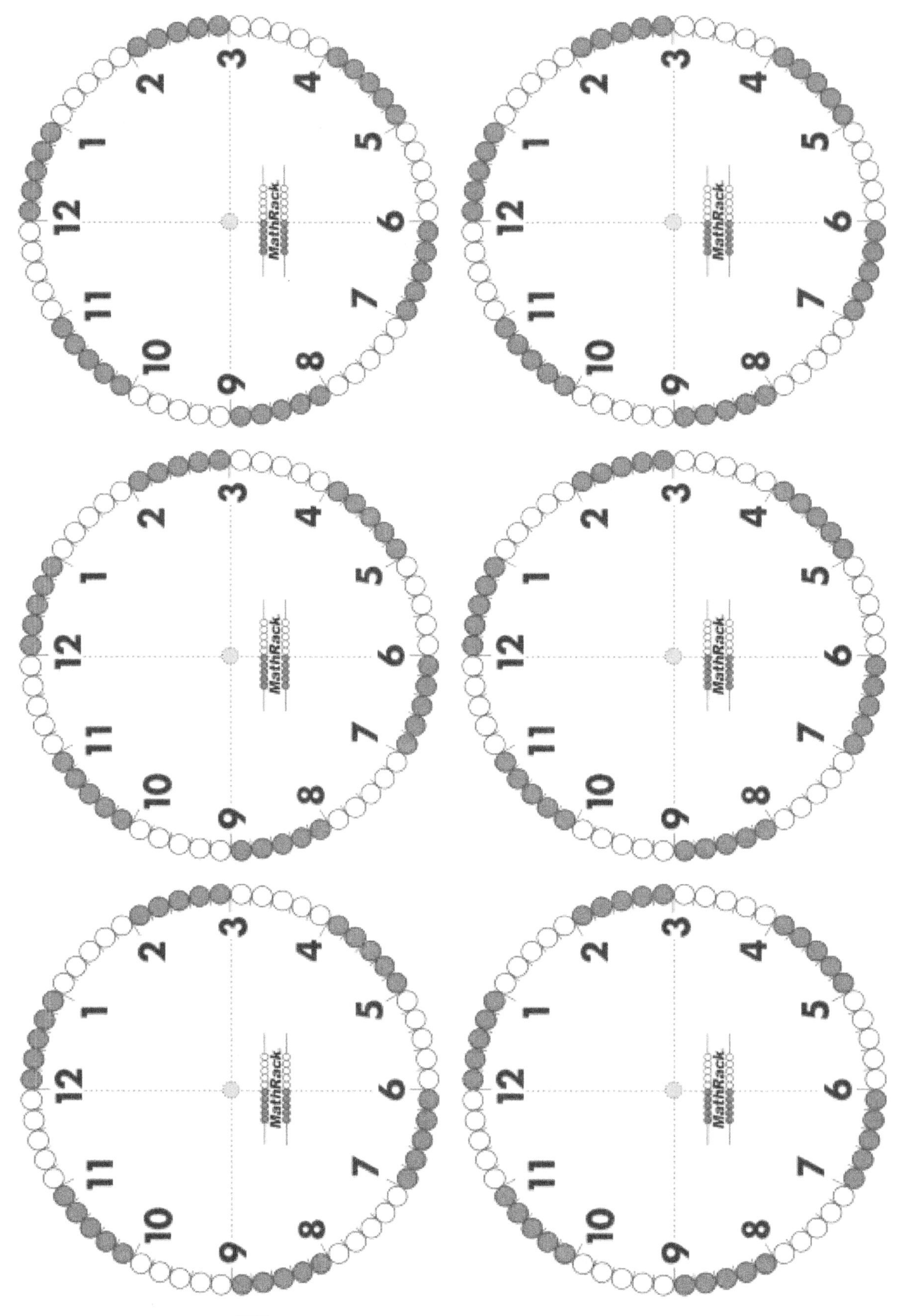

Appendix H—Clock Cards for Playing *What Time is It?* (3 of 4)

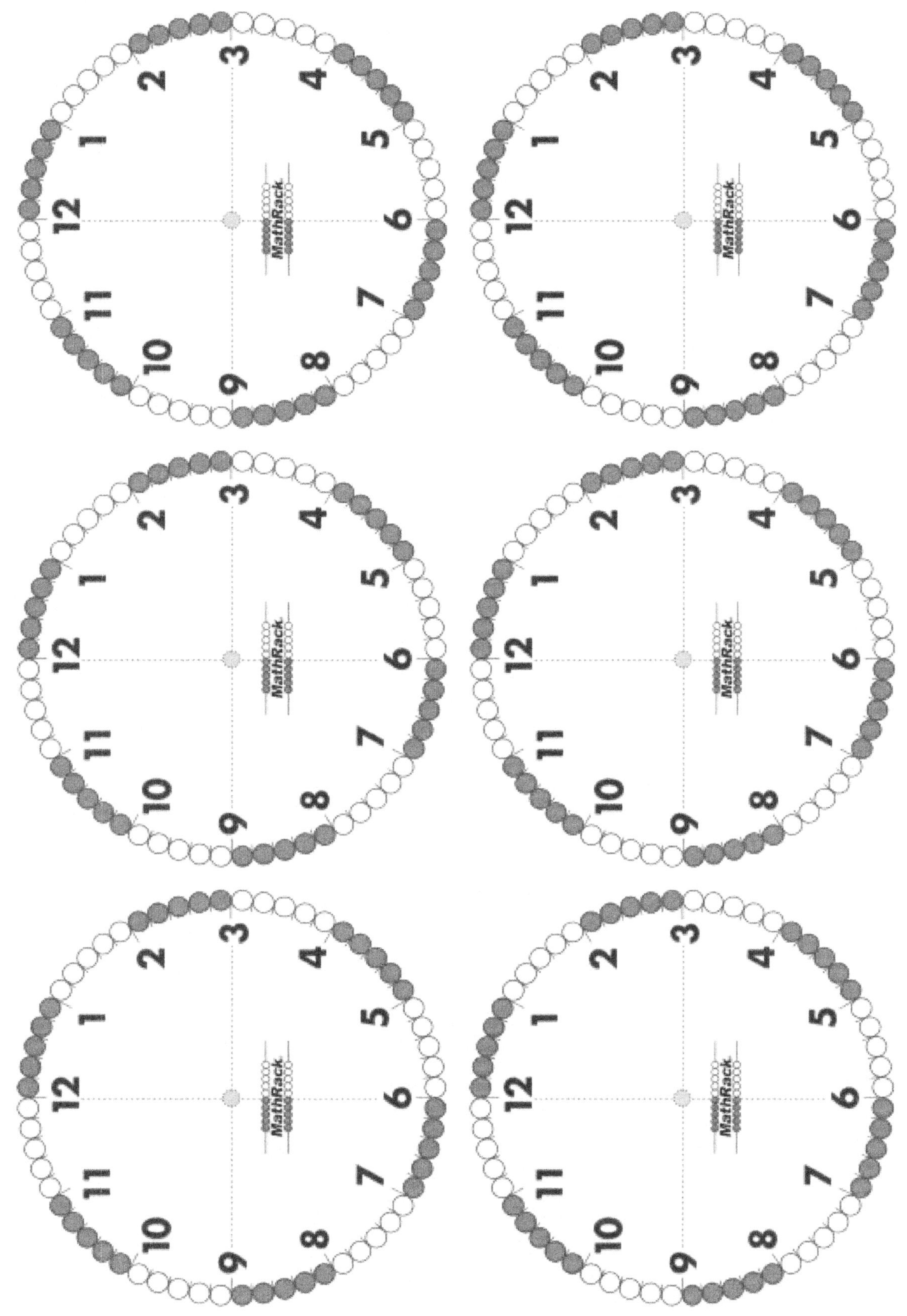

Appendix H—Clock Cards for Playing *What Time is It?* (4 of 4)

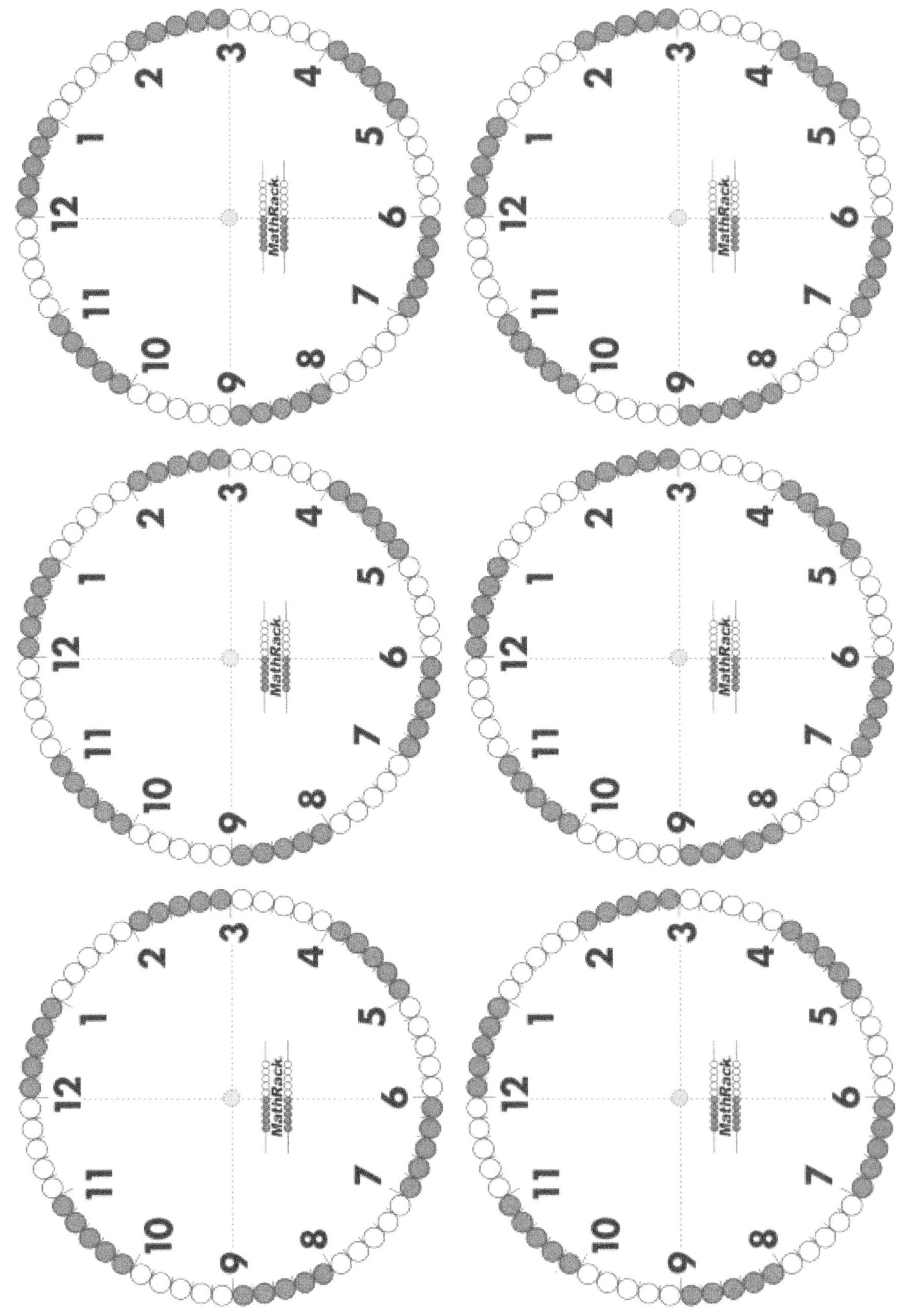

Appendix I—Blank Clock Faces

Made in the USA
Monee, IL
15 June 2023

35844680R00031